20 Peace Lessons from Northern Ireland to Israel and Palestine

Also by Colin Irwin

The People's Peace Process in Northern Ireland

The People's Peace: 'Pax Populi, Pax Dei'-
    How Peace Polls are Democratizing The Peace Making Process

For articles, reports and updates see the authors website at:

www.peacepolls.org

20 Peace Lessons
from Northern Ireland to
Israel and Palestine

Colin Irwin

20 Peace Lessons
from Northern Ireland to
Israel and Palestine

First edition 2012
Printed in the United States of America

ISBN-13: 978-1478382317
ISBN-10: 1478382317

This edition is printed on demand by
CreateSpace, Scotts Valley, CA.

For the peacemakers

Contents

List of Figures

List of Tables

Glossary and Abbreviations

Anglo-Irish Agreement – Signed by the British and Irish governments in November 1985

Articles 2 and 3 – Articles in the 1937 Irish Constitution which laid claim to the six counties of Northern Ireland

Belfast Agreement – Signed by the British and Irish governments in April 1998 and otherwise known as the Good Friday Agreement (GFA)

BBC – British Broadcasting Corporation

Clinton Parameters – A set of guidelines for a Permanent Status Agreement to resolve the Israel-Palestine conflict in late 2000

Direct Rule – From Westminster over Northern Ireland and introduced in 1972 following the suspension of Stormont

Downing Street Declaration – Proposals for a Northern Ireland settlement published by the British and Irish governments in December 1993

DUP – Democratic Unionist Party

EC/EU - European Community/European Union

Framework Document – Proposals for a Northern Ireland settlement published by the British and Irish governments in February 1995

Geneva Accord – A refinement of the Clinton Parameters and other proposals to resolve the Israel-Palestine conflict in 2003

IDF – Israel Defence Force

IDPs – Internally Displaced Persons

IGO – Inter-governmental Organisation

IIASR – Israel Institute of Applied Social Research

IICD – Independent International Commission on Decommissioning

IOCRI – Israel and Palestine Centre for Research and Information

IRA – Irish Republican Army also referred to as the Provisional IRA formed after a split with the Official IRA in 1969

JMCC – Jerusalem Media and Communication Centre

JRCT – Joseph Rowntree Charitable Trust

LVF – Loyalist Volunteer Force

Mitchell Principles – Six conditions for inclusive political discussions contained in the Mitchell Report of February 1996

NGO – Non-governmental Organisation

NIO – Northern Ireland Office

NIWC – Northern Ireland Women's Coalition

Oslo Accords – Israeli and Palestinian Declaration of Principles on Interim Self-Government Arrangements signed in Washington September 1993

Patten Report – Commission report on reform of the RUC published in 1999

PA – Palestinian Authority

PASSIA – Palestinian Academic Society for the Study of International Affairs

PCPSR – Palestinian Centre for Policy and Survey Research

PR – Proportional representation

PUP – Progressive Unionist Party

RUC – Royal Ulster Constabulary

SDLP – Social Democratic and Labour Party

SF - Sinn Féin

UDA – Ulster Defence Association

UDP – Ulster Democratic Party

UFF – Ulster Freedom Fighters

UKUP – United Kingdom Unionist Party

UN – United Nations

UUP – Ulster Unionist Party

UVF – Ulster Volunteer Force

WAPOR – World Association of Public Opinion Research

Acknowledgements

This book is a product of the peace lessons learnt through two programs of research, one in Northern Ireland and the other in Israel and Palestine. It is not possible to thank all those who gave their time so generously to these projects so I will just mention some of the key people here from each area of research:

In Palestine: Mahdi Abdul Hadi of the Palestinian Academic Society for the Study of International Affairs, Ghassan Khatib of the Jerusalem Media and Communications Centre, Nader Said at Arab World for Research and Development and Nisreen Shahin of OneVoice.

In Israel: Louis Guttman, Eliu Katz and Haviva Bar at the Israel Institute of Applied Social Research, Mina Zemach at Dahaf, and Gil Shamey of OneVoice.

In Northern Ireland: Terrance Flanagan, Brian Lambkin, Cecilia Linehan, Billy Hutchinson, Dawn Pervis, David Ervine, David Adams, Garey McMichael, Jim Gibney, Gerry ó hEára, Conor Murphy, Mark Durkan, Sean Farran, Alban Maginness, Barbara McCabe, Kate Fearon, Stephen Farry, Hugh Casey, Alan Evans, Peter Weir, Jim Wilson, Graham Gudgion, Ian Paisley Jr., John Cobain, Jeffrey Dudgeon, Edmund Curren, David Neely, Chris Moffat, Graham Gingles, David Pozorski, Bill Nolan, Steven Pittam, David Shutt and Alan Leich at Market Research Northern Ireland as well as George Munroe and Christine Cahoon who maintain my website at www.peacepolls.org.

I must also thank those who provided me with the necessary institutional and academic support to undertake the research:

At The Queens University of Belfast: John Blacking, Reginald Byron, Elisabeth Tonkin, Brian Walker, Fred Boal, Tom Hadden, Steven Livingstone, PL de Silva, Adrian Guelke, Mrs Gracey, Anne Langford, Tom Collins and Senator George Mitchell when he was the Chancellor.

At the University of Ulster: Brice Dickson.

At The University of Liverpool: Marianne Elliott and Jonathan Tonge.

I must also extend my gratitude to the governments, institutions, agencies and charities who provided me with a base from which to work and paid all the bills. They were: The Social Science and Humanities Research Council of Canada, the Central Community Relations Unit of the

Northern Ireland Office, The Joseph Rowntree Charitable Trust, The Queen's University of Belfast (in particular the Department of Anthropology, School of Law and Institute of Irish Studies), Atlantic Philanthropies, The Queen's University of Belfast Foundation, The University of Liverpool (in particular the Institute of Irish Studies and the Department of Politics), the British Academy and Royal Norwegian Ministry of Foreign Affairs.

My professional organisation the World Association of Public Opinion Research must also be thanked for their support in particular their founder Sir Robert Worcestor and Past Presidents Hans Zetterberg and Michael Traugott.

Lastly I must thank my daughter Melissa and partner Hae-kyung Um for their tolerance and continued encouragement to pursue my work.

Preface

I first went to Israel in 1968 just after the 67' War and for six months worked as a diving instructor at the Red Sea resort of Eilat. It was largely my experiences as a young man in this country that prompted me to make a career of peace studies. With a post-doctoral fellowship from the Canadian government I returned to Israel in 1987 to complete a comparative study of the processes of social integration amongst Eastern and Western Jewish children who went to school together in Jerusalem and Catholic and Protestant Christian children who went to school together in Belfast.[1] The study was done using a Smallest Space Analysis programme developed for this purpose[2] at the Israel Institute of Applied Social Research (IIASR). Given the greater cultural differences of Jewish children migrating to Israel from very different parts of the world we discovered the children in Belfast were integrating better than the children in Jerusalem.

Between April 1996 and February 2003 I conducted nine surveys of public opinion in support of the Northern Ireland peace process. Critically the questions for eight of these polls were drafted and agreed with the co-operation of party negotiators to enhance the peace process by increasing party inclusiveness, developing issues and language, testing party policies, helping to set deadlines and increase the overall transparency of negotiations through the publication of technical analysis and media

---

[1] Irwin, C. J., How Integrated Education Works, in *Education Together for a Change: Integrated Education and Community Relations in Northern Ireland*, Ed. C. Moffat, Fortnight Educational Trust, Belfast, (1993). Irwin, C. J., Integrated Education: From Theory to Practice in Divided Societies, *Prospects*, UNESCO Quarterly Review of Education. Vol. XXII, No.1, (English Edition, ISSN 0033-1538, UNESCO; French Edition, ISSN 0304-3045, UNESCO; Spanish Edition, ISSN 0304-3052, UNESCO; Arabic Edition, ISSN 0254-119-X, UNESCO; Russian Edition, ISSN 0207-8953, Moscow; Chinese Edition, ISSN 0254-8682, Beijing), UNESCO Paris, January, ((1992).
[2] Irwin, C. J., and Bar, H., 'Israel and Northern Ireland' in Irwin, C. J., *Education and the Development of Social Integration in Divided Societies*, Northern Ireland Council For Integrated Education, Belfast, August, (1991).

reports. The work was a great success as was the peace process.[3]

Following the conclusion of the Belfast Agreement in 1998 and the 'Mitchell Review' of the Agreement in 1999, Atlantic Philanthropies awarded me a two-year fellowship in 2000 to explore the possibilities of applying the methods developed there internationally. With the assistance of this grant, which I had received with the support of Senator George Mitchell, I made arrangements to visit Jerusalem again in 2002, and it soon became clear that a group of suitable people could be brought together to design and run polls similar to those undertaken in Northern Ireland.

Naomi Chazan, who was then the Deputy Speaker of the Knesset and a past Director of the Truman Institute for the Advancement of Peace, as well as Ghassan Khatib, Director of the Jerusalem Media and Communication Centre (JMCC) and who later become a Minister in the Palestinian Authority (PA), Vice President of Birzeit University and Director of the Government Media Centre, both expressed a keen interest in such a project. At the time the Director of the Palestinian Academic Society for the Study of International Affairs (PASSIA), Mahdi Abdul Hadi, was particularly interested in running a poll that explored the possibilities for elections in the occupied territories. Some questions were drafted, and with the support of the French government he was to fly to Paris to examine these issues further but when his colleagues were stopped at Israeli checkpoints and prevented from joining him at the airport, the project was brought to a close and elections were not held until after Arafat's death in 2004. Freedom of association and freedom of expression are minimum requirements for this kind of peace research, and these conditions could not be adequately met to complete our project at that time.

Between 2002 and 2008 I completed a program of peace polls across the Balkans in Macedonia, Bosnia and Herzegovina, Kosovo and Serbia followed by a series of peace polls in Kashmir and Sri Lanka.[4] I returned to Israel and Palestine whenever I could but had to wait until Barack Obama was elected to the White House and George Mitchell was appointed his Special Envoy to the Middle East before I was invited to undertake a peace poll there. Unfortunately, this effort at peace making proved to be 'too little, too late', the peace process failed and George Mitchell resigned his position in 2011.

---

[3] Irwin, C. J., *The People's Peace Process in Northern Ireland*, Palgrave MacMillan, Basingstoke and New York, (2002).
[4] Irwin, C. J., *The People's Peace: 'Pax Populi, Pax Dei' - How Peace Polls are Democratizing the Peace Making Process*, CreateSpace, Scotts Valley, CA, (2012).

All conflicts are different, different peoples, places, cultures, languages, religions, histories etc. etc. So the solutions needed to resolve these conflicts are also necessarily very different. Specifically, the political arrangements for the resolution of the Northern Ireland conflict contained in the Belfast Agreement are very different to the proposed arrangements for ending the Israel Palestine conflict. However, the road to peace, the steps that have to be taken to get to peace, the peace process itself is quite another matter and in this regard there is a very great deal that the world can learn from Northern Ireland. This book is written to detail 20 such lessons for Israel and Palestine.

Introduction

Effective peace building requires the reestablishment of all those elements of a society that make it a functioning success. In the first instance an absence of dialogue between the conflicting parties must be replaced with reliable channels of communication that can facilitate an honest discourse on all the issues that lie at the heart of the conflict. Secondly, once the talking has begun in earnest, discussion must lead to real negotiations and decision making on each element of an agreement that provides remedies for every failed social practice and inoperative political institution. Finally, once the agreement is reached it must be implemented in full, with as much rigour, care and attention to success as the negotiations themselves. Peace building and peace making requires both vigilance and patience and in this the support of all of the elements of the society and the international community must be encouraged to play a constructive role if a return to violence and war is to be avoided.

In Northern Ireland public opinion polls were used to enhance all of these essential processes by helping to establish real dialogue and effective communications; explore problems and their solutions; define the critical issues and associated questions and last, but by no means least, help to keep the peace process on track by facilitating a discourse in which the society as a whole could play a part in the decision making process.

There are also things that public opinion polls should not be used for in peace processes. Regrettably they can be designed to undermine the efforts of peace builders when they are employed by one party to a conflict to advance their own agenda while ignoring the concerns of others. Questions can also be designed to create distrust and even despair by addressing just the problems and not their solutions or by highlighting the fears and prejudices of each community while ignoring the hopes and aspirations of the society to move beyond the failures of the past.

Those who have a vested interest in a continuation of the status quo can also use public opinion polls to undo the good that may have been done by attempting to undermine and/or renegotiate agreements by selectively revisiting the concessions that only one side, their side, has made. Responsible editors and journalists should avoid all of these temptations often embarked upon to grab a headline and create disagreement in an effort to increase circulation, ratings and sales. But responsible editors and journalists, politicians and academics can do otherwise. They can use public opinion polls to help build peace and, step-by-step, the successes of the Northern Ireland experience points the way to how this can be done.

Of course the Northern Ireland experience is also littered with failure. Some things worked and some things didn't. But the purpose of this book is to review, with all the benefits of hindsight, the things that did work in the hope that others can learn from that experience. Regrettably these lessons have not been learnt in Israel and Palestine, or if they have been learnt then they have been deliberately ignored.

It may be possible to simply manage the conflict in the Middle East for some years to come but the world requires that this conflict is resolved. Best practice in Northern Ireland peace making can bring all the parties much closer to that objective and to this end the 20 peace lessons critically reviewed here are divided into three main categories as follows:

1. Establishing real dialogue and effective communication
2. Problems, solutions, questions, issues and language
3. Keeping the peace process 'on track'

Establishing Real Dialogue and Effective Communication

Lesson 1 – Inter-track dialogue and diplomacy

Peace Building Problem
All too often political parties find they have to align themselves with different sections of society and communities to get elected. In deeply divided societies this reality can lead to the increased polarisation of party policies and their associated electorate groups[5] when most people, most of the time, would prefer accommodation, peace and the prosperity that flows from political stability. All too often politicians and political parties (track one) find it difficult, if not impossible, to establish a positive dialogue with all the people (track three) through the media and institutions of civil society (track two) in an effort to define a set of common goals with a view to achieving some common ends.

Northern Ireland Experience
Public opinion polls were used in Northern Ireland to create a form of inter-track diplomacy through an on-going process of questionnaire design with the politicians, interviews with their electorate and publication of survey results in the local press. This did not happen 'over night' by way of some carefully designed diplomatic strategy but over a period of months and years during which time all the elements of this peace building exercise were put into place. Firstly, a programme of pure research was undertaken by a group of academics at The Queen's University of Belfast[6] on different aspects of peace building and public policy that included a public opinion poll survey and the publication of the findings in a series of articles in the *Belfast Telegraph*[7] and as a supplement in a local current

---

[5] D. L. Horowitz, *Ethnic Groups in Conflict*. (Berkeley: University of California Press, 1985).
[6] T. Hadden, C. Irwin and F. Boal, 'Separation or sharing? the people's choice', Supplement with *Fortnight* 356, Belfast, December, (1996).
[7] C. J. Irwin, 'STILL POLLS APART, People longing for real talks to start', *Belfast Telegraph*, Wednesday, April 9th, (1997). C. J. Irwin, 'Referendums could bypass politicians', *Belfast Telegraph*, Wednesday, April 9th, (1997). C. J. Irwin, 'DRUMCREE THREE, Rule of law is what people of Northern Ireland want', *Belfast Telegraph*, Tuesday, April 8th, (1997). C. J. Irwin, 'Wide support for Bill of Rights', *Belfast Telegraph*, Tuesday, April 8th, (1997). C. J. Irwin, 'TRUCE HOLDS KEY, Sharp divisions on how talks replace the guns', *Belfast Telegraph*, Monday, April 7th, (1997). C. J. Irwin, 'Voter's query parties' push', *Belfast Telegraph*, Monday, April 7th, (1997). C. J. Irwin, 'Few believe peace is at hand', *Belfast Telegraph*, Monday, April 7th, (1997).

affairs magazine, *Fortnight*.[8] This study also included questions that began to explore attitudes towards various political solutions to the Northern Ireland problem. Secondly, the political parties elected to participate in the negotiations on the future of Northern Ireland were invited and agreed to participate in the drafting of a new poll designed to address all the issues presently holding up progress in the negotiations. They agreed providing individuals were not cited as being actively involved in the exercise. A degree of discretion was essential especially when 'old enemies' were co-operating in a common enterprise. Thirdly, funding was secured from an independent sponsor, the Joseph Rowntree Charitable Trust, that all parties accepted as neutral and agreement was reached with the *Belfast Telegraph* that their paper would publish the reports of the surveys without insisting on editorial control of their content. The political consultations, interviews, analysis, writing and publication were genuinely independent, from beginning to end, across all three tracks of the process. Consequently the parties had confidence in the process and took the results of the research seriously.

Peace Making Best Practice
Get the media, newspapers, political parties, appropriate charities and sponsors, universities and academics involved in a collective enterprise of designing and running a series of public opinion polls as part of a peace process.

Israel and Palestine
In the name of security the government of Israel has erected both physical and legal barriers that make interactions between the peacemakers on both sides extremely difficult and sometimes quite impossible. Informal interactions between journalists, editors, academics, researchers and politicians are severely restricted between the two communities. As a consequence of these policies the polling work undertaken in Israel and Palestine is frequently dominated by single community partisan agendas that emphasise problems rather than solutions. Without the right to the freedom of association between the committed peacemakers on both sides and the proactive encouragement for them to exercise that right civil society can never become an effective partner for peace. Jerusalem was once the centre for all such interactions and should be again through the lifting of all restrictions that bar peacemakers from the city of peace.

---

[8] T. Hadden, C. Irwin and F. Boal, 'Separation or sharing? the people's choice', Supplement with *Fortnight* 356, Belfast, December, (1996).

Lesson 2 - The formation of a contact group to help resolve the conflict

Peace Building Problem
Political parties, who are at best electoral competitors and at worst actively engaged in hostilities publicly refuse to enter into negotiations with their 'enemies' without first having them agree to a series of unacceptable preconditions. But without dialogue any possibility of achieving a workable agreement on the preconditions, let alone a settlement of the conflict, is impossible - the ultimate 'chicken and egg' problem.

Northern Ireland Experience
Although the first purely academic piece of research demonstrated public support for a political compromise on the future of Northern Ireland the politicians disagreed with a lot of what was done in this poll. Many of them thought the questions were biased or were the wrong questions on the wrong issues or even that the most important issues had been ignored. Inevitably different politicians from different parties had very different views on these matters. Some of them also thought that the methodology could be improved in terms of the way the questions were asked, analysed or broken down in terms of community and political groups. These criticisms were all very healthy, welcome and provided for a great deal to talk about and agree upon without running the risk of making political decisions that were irreversible. Through a series of private interviews with representatives of each party firstly the issues to be dealt with in the next poll were agreed as well as the time when they thought it could most effectively be published. Secondly the introduction to the polling interview was agreed in which it was clearly stated who was doing the research, who was funding it and who would get the results. Thirdly successive drafts of the questions were circulated until a consensus was reached in which each party felt their issues were dealt with to their satisfaction and that no other parties issues were put forward unfairly with questions that would be considered leading. In this way, informally, quick progress was made on a wide range of issues that were not necessarily being discussed in the formal negotiations at that time because of procedural and/or agenda problems. When the results of the first poll were published a number of procedural problems were solved and both the negotiations proper and the private polls were able to move on to the next set of issues - the different parts of an agreement.

Peace Making Best Practice

Firstly, run a public opinion poll that demonstrates the desire of the people for an honourable settlement and that the possibility of achieving an agreement is real. Secondly, invite all the serious parties to the conflict to appoint a representative to work with the researchers on designing and agreeing a series of public opinion polls with the expressed objective of assisting the parties with their negotiations.

Israel and Palestine

With the election of President Obama to the White House in November 2008 and the appointment of Senator George Mitchell as his Special Envoy to the Middle East in 2009 a peace poll was conducted in Israel and Palestine that clearly demonstrated the possibility of achieving a peace agreement.[9] Many other polls had confirmed this reality over the years.[10] But that is as far as the process went. Instead of using the results of the peace poll to deal constructively with problems in the negotiations the Israelis used partisan polls and public diplomacy to oppose a balanced set of accommodations that would have seen the negotiations move forward.[11] Regrettably funding for the peace polls was then terminated, so an invitation to engage with Israeli political parties more clearly committed to achieving a peace agreement with the Palestinians could not be made, and the peace process failed.[12] In these circumstances peace-making must not be restricted to government parties alone but extended to all politicians dedicated to achieving an end to conflict.

---

[9] Irwin, C. J., Israel and Palestine: Public Opinion, Public Diplomacy and Peace Making. Part 1. The Shape of an Agreement, Part 2. Process, *www.Peacepolls.org*, April, (2009).

[10] Shamir, J. and Shikaki, K., *Palestinian and Israeli Public Opinion: The Public Imperative in the Second Intifada*, Indiana University Press, Bloomington and Indianapolis, (2010).

[11] Irwin, C. J., Israel and Palestine Peace Polls: Public Opinion and Peace Making in Comparative Perspective, *Public Opinion and Survey Research in a Changing World*, WAPOR Annual Conference, September 11th to 13th, Lausanne, Switzerland, (2009).

[12] Irwin, C. J., *The People's Peace: Pax Populi, Pax Dei - How Peace Polls are Democratizing the Peace Making Process*, CreateSpace, Scotts Valley, CA, (2012).

Lesson 3 - Establishing confidential lines of communication between the parties to a conflict

Peace Building Problem
A break down of communication due to a lack of trust. For example when parties engaged in hostilities will not give up violence in favour of political negotiations because they do not believe the other parties will negotiate in good faith. When, perhaps, one party or the other believes the negotiations and/or the cease-fire is only tactical.

Northern Ireland Experience
When the negotiations for the first poll were begun in January 1997 the Conservatives were in government in Westminster where they relied on the votes of the Northern Ireland Unionists to keep them in power. In this situation the possibility of meaningful compromises being agreed on the future of the Province were very doubtful and consequently the Irish Republican Army (IRA) had broken their cease-fire and returned to hostilities against the British state. In these circumstances there was a break down of effective communications between Sinn Féin (the political wing of the IRA) and the other political parties, the two governments and the Office of the Independent Chairmen because the British were opposed to any negotiations with terrorists at war. When Labour replaced the Conservatives in May 1997 Sinn Féin wanted to reinstate their cease-fire and return to political negotiations but only if they believed that these negotiations would be undertaken in good faith. They wanted to be sure that those responsible for managing the talks would not allow the Unionists, in particular Dr Paisley the leader of the Democratic Unionist Party, to frustrate progress through filibusters and other delaying tactics. In particular they were concerned to know how Senator George Mitchell, the senior talks chairman, might handle such matters. These concerns were addressed to Sinn Féin's satisfaction firstly through the informal channels of communication available to them, which included the public opinion poll contact group, and then formally when the embargo on direct communication with the British government was temporarily lifted during an informal suspension of hostilities. Subsequently the IRA called their second cease-fire, the DUP left the talks, the Ulster Unionists did not block progress and the Belfast Agreement was signed on Good Friday 1998. As an academic at Queen's University the poll facilitator also had free access to other scholars, in particular human rights and constitutional lawyers, who were able to give opinions on specific issues when a party to the negotiations so required.

Peace Making Best Practice

Establish independent, reliable and confidential lines of communication between the parties with points of access to other independent third parties who can provide expert advice as required.

Israel and Palestine

Because the negotiations between Israel and Palestine are limited to the parties in government, independents and small parties who may be strongly pro-peace (e.g. Meretz in Israel) or parties very sceptical of the value of negotiations (e.g. Hamas in Palestine) become side-lined by the peace process. At the very least they should be part of informal contact groups so that they can make a positive contribution to negotiations when they are able to do so and/or become a party to a final settlement if and when it might be achieved. Of course they may not take advantage of such opportunities but through informal contact groups, that include common programs of public opinion research, all the parties have the opportunity to communicate with each other, share their ideas and concerns and thus vicariously be a party to a peace process that may, from time to time, break down at the formal level.

Lesson 4 - Establishing confidence in the peace process

Peace Building Problem
After years of violence, 'off again - on again' war and numerous failed political initiatives to bring the conflict to an end very few people have any confidence that yet another attempt to conclude an agreement will be any more successful than all the failures of the past.

Northern Ireland Experience
In addition to all the sophisticated questions designed to map out the structure and elements of a peace agreement a few simple 'Yes/No' questions were included in each of the Northern Ireland polls with the intention of creating a confidence-building headline in the local press. Consequently on the front page of the *Belfast Telegraph* of 7 April 1997[13] under the banner headline 'YOUR VERDICT' sub headlines from the first poll also read '94% Want a negotiated settlement' as well as '69% Do not want talks to stop' but also more soberly '74% Believe Stormont talks will fail'. In the second poll on 11 September 1997[14] the headline was '92% SAY YES' to the question 'Do you want your party to stay in the talks?' and the editorial leader was entitled ''Yes' to talks'. Additionally 'Put talks package to vote' was the front-page story the following day on 12 September[15] with the observation that 'Less than one in ten - 9% - regard the idea as unacceptable'. The third poll moved on from questions of procedure and started to deal with the substance of a settlement so that on 12 January 1998[16] the front page story was 'Poll signals backing for new assembly', on 13 January[17] it was 'NORTH SOUTH LINKS VERDICT' and on 14 January[18] the front page story was 'Poll reveals Ulster yes for islands council'. Before the agreement was signed it was tested in the fourth poll. On 31 March 1998[19] the banner headline was '77% SAY YES' and the deal was finally struck on Good Friday. But that wasn't the end of

---

[13] M. Simpson, 'YOUR VERDICT', *Belfast Telegraph*, Monday, April 7th, (1997).
[14] M. Simpson, '92% SAY YES', *Belfast Telegraph*, Thursday September 11th, (1998).
[15] M. Simpson, 'Put talks package to vote', *Belfast Telegraph*, Friday September 12th, (1998).
[16] Political Staff, 'Poll signals backing for new assembly', *Belfast Telegraph*, Monday, January 12th, (1998).
[17] M. Purdy, 'NORTH - SOUTH LINKS VERDICT', *Belfast Telegraph*, Tuesday, January 17th, (1998).
[18] N. McAdam, 'Poll reveals Ulster yes for islands council', *Belfast Telegraph*, Wednesday, January 14th, (1998).
[19] P. Connolly, '77% SAY YES', *Belfast Telegraph*, Tuesday, March 31st, (1998).

the matter. Implementation became a problem with Unionists wanting 'guns before government' and Republicans wanting 'government before guns'. On 3 March 1999[20] the front page story was 'DUP voters want deal to work: poll' and the inside page was '93% SAY: MAKE THE AGREEMENT WORK'. But it didn't work all that summer so with Senator Mitchell as facilitator everyone tried again. By 26 October[21] the *Belfast Telegraph* front page headline now read '65% STILL FOR DEAL' - that is to say they would still vote 'Yes' while 85 per cent still wanted the agreement to work. Support was not as strong as it was but as the editorial pointed out on that day it was 'Still the best option'. Confidence was maintained.

Peace Making Best Practice
Although the public opinion polls must deal with all the problems and possible solutions that lie at the heart of a conflict questions of confidence and continued progress should also be addressed by asking people if they want a political agreement, an end to violence, negotiations to be started, timely decisions to be made, democratic institutions to be re-established, the maintenance of human rights standards and the rule of law, effective policing acceptable to the whole community and economic development in the context of peace and so on. Of course nearly everyone wants all these things and asking such questions, arguably, is a trivial use of the polls. But providing such questions are only included in the context of the more serious issues that must be addressed then giving 'a boost' to the self confidence of both the politicians and their electorate, from time to time, can be a very worth while thing to do in an effort to provide some encouragement to the war weary population.

Israel and Palestine
The people of Israel and Palestine are war weary, occupation weary and fruitless negotiations weary. The Israelis want security and the Palestinians want their own state so asking any question regarding a desire to achieve these goals, to end the conflict and establish the means to do so, will inevitably get a positive response. The Israeli and Palestinian media should be full of public exaltations for their politicians to do what they should do – negotiate and conclude a peace agreement. But the polls run in Israel and Palestine rarely do this – why? Firstly it is only worthwhile to do so when

---

[20] M. Purdy, 'DUP voters want deal to work: poll', *Belfast Telegraph*, Wednesday March 3rd, (1999).
[21] N. McAdam, '65% STILL FOR DEAL', *Belfast Telegraph*, Tuesday, October 26th, (1999).

the peace process is active. If the prospect of progress is zero then there is no point in building up the people's hopes only to get them shattered. Secondly, and more commonly, failed politicians prefer negative headlines that emphasise the public expectation that they will indeed fail. So expectations get polled while desires get ignored to give these failed politicians an opportunity to say 'the people did not think that this process would work anyway'. Expectation questions should never be asked in isolation. They are run for the benefit of these failed politicians who expect or may even want a failed peace process. The media will inevitably run such questions that underline the negative expectations of their publics so peace polls must always counter such questions by running them alongside questions that emphasise the people's desires for peace process success.

Problems, Solutions, Questions, Issues and Language

Lesson 5 - Formulating the policies needed for conflict resolution

Peace Building Problem
Exploring all the possible elements of compromise and accommodation in public may be seen as weakness and open up a party's negotiating position to attacks from more radical elements and/or political opportunists.

Northern Ireland Experience
The parties elected to take part in the negotiation of the Belfast Agreement frequently found themselves in a complex of 'Catch 22' traps. If a major Unionist, Loyalist, Nationalist or Republican party suggested a creative and bold compromise they would be attacked as traitors by members of their own community opposed to the peace process. But if they said nothing then they appeared to be doing nothing even if, behind closed doors, secret negotiations were taking place in earnest. Unfortunately such secret negotiations allowed for the creation of mischievous rumours and falsified leaked documents which were generally far more radical in their content than the negotiations proper. Both honest open debate and discrete private discussions opened up a party to political attack. Those opposed to an agreement worked very hard to make sure all possible solutions to the Northern Ireland problem 'spelt disaster' in the public mind before they had a chance of becoming a reality. To deal with this problem the parties developed an unwritten 'code of practice' for running the public opinion polls that involved the following key features:

- All questions and options had to be introduced by a party to the negotiations to ensure both relevance and serious intent.
- The wording had to be agreed by all the parties to the negotiations to remove bias, leading or partisan phrasing.
- Questions and options could not be attributed to a party in public or in private communications. The detailed footnotes that accompanied each draft questionnaire made no reference to party connections and the notes on attribution, that accompanied each newspaper report, were agreed with all the parties and were generally vague on this particular point.

Peace Making Best Practice
Test all the possible elements of compromise and accommodation proposed as various options in a public opinion poll without attributing the different options to any particular party.

Israel and Palestine

Public opinion and public diplomacy is not managed to help Israel and Palestine get to peace. Arguably, from a post Northern Ireland perspective, this is not a modern peace process. The parties to this conflict do not use public opinion research to systematically explore solutions that could resolve the problems that are holding up negotiations. If surveys of public opinion were not a regular part of the political culture of Israel and Palestine this situation would be understandable but this is not the case. Louis Guttman who founded the Israel Institute of Applied Social Research (IIASR) in 1955 pioneered a program of regular polling in both Israel and Palestine following the 67 War. Israel and Palestine were the first state/people to be surveyed in this way with a view to resolving their conflict. Regrettably this expertise has not been developed and used constructively to achieve peace in recent years by building on the lessons of Northern Ireland.

Lesson 6 - Setting the agenda and 'getting past go'

Peace Building Problem

Each party to a conflict want their particular agenda dealt with first, preferably, if at all possible, as a precondition to the negotiations proper. Such rigidity can stall negotiations in the pre-negotiation agenda setting stage so no one 'gets off first base'.

Northern Ireland Experience

The Unionists took the view that several of the issues that were part of the agenda for the Stormont talks should not be items for negotiation at all because they were in breach of domestic UK or international European law. In particular Unionists believed decommissioning of paramilitary weapons, particularly those belonging to the IRA, and the removal of the Irish claim over the territory of Northern Ireland, in Articles 2 and 3 of their constitution, were not matters for negotiation. Rather they felt these issues should be settled to the satisfaction of Unionists before the negotiations proper for a power sharing assembly, North/South bodies, police reform and so on. Republicans and Nationalists accepted none of this. They believed Unionists would negotiate no further once they had got what they wanted on these critical points. The talks were stalled and several questions were written specifically to address these problems. For example, in the poll published in the *Belfast Telegraph* on 11 September 1997,[22] 65 per cent of Protestants considered it 'unacceptable' to stay in the talks with Sinn Féin if their cease-fire broke down while only 12 per cent of Catholics shared this view. On the other hand 52 per cent of Catholics considered it 'unacceptable' to make decommissioning a talks precondition while only 16 per cent of Protestants agreed (Table 1). The solution to this apparently intractable dilemma was the establishment of the Independent International Commission on Decommissioning to deal with the problem while the talks were in progress. Opinions were also split on when to deal with the problem of Articles 2 and 3 of the Irish Constitution. But this issue was not so critical as the question of decommissioning. Only 17 per cent of Protestants and 3 per cent of Catholics considered it 'unacceptable' not to 'Keep the Talks going' on this occasion and 'let reform of the Republic of Ireland's Constitution be dealt with at the same time as all the other issues that must be part of an over all settlement'. This is what happened.

---

[22] C. J. Irwin, 'YES vote for talks', *Belfast Telegraph*, Thursday, September 11th, (1997).

Table 1. All the parties should be prepared to talk to each other...

Percentage 'Unacceptable'	Protestant	Catholic
Even if the cease-fires do not hold.	65	12
So long as the cease-fires hold.	16	8
So long as the cease-fires hold and there is also some decommissioning.	10	17
Only after decommissioning has been completed.	16	52

Peace Making Best Practice
Test proposals for precondition items against public opinion. When 'we' do not want 'their' issues dealt with before 'ours' and 'they' do not want 'our' issues dealt with before 'theirs' the only option that will gain the widest cross community support will be for all issues to be dealt with at the same time without any preconditions. However, on many occasions, both communities will actually prefer negotiations to go ahead without any preconditions or delays at all, particularly if the issue is not critical to their safety or security.

Israel and Palestine
Negotiations between Israel and Palestine are not 'getting past go' because of the settlement issue. Palestinians are not asking for the removal of illegal settlements before negotiations can start, or the removal of checkpoints or an end to occupation. Their bottom line is simply no more settlement expansion during negotiations. Israelis want an end to rocket attacks from Gaza. The Palestinians have been able to arrange such cease-fires in the past so a quid pro quo poll that explores all such possibilities in a balanced way should produce a positive result with no more breaches of international law on either side. Such a poll that examines every conceivable precondition from both a Palestinian and Israeli point of view, however extreme and unreasonable, has never been run because, in a peace poll, the utter reasonableness of balanced accommodations tied only to negotiations would inevitably come through as the logical choice.[23] Faced with such a threat to the status quo Israel was allowed to engage in a program of partisan polling that focused on the views of the settlers and the peace process, under the stewardship of Senator George Mitchell, was brought to an untimely close. Such errors of public diplomacy can be fatal and should not be repeated.[24]

---

[23] For a preliminary analysis of these peace process solutions see the Irwin/OneVoice 2009 peace poll *Israel and Palestine: Public Opinion, Public Diplomacy and Peace Making* available at www.peacepolls.org.
[24] For a review of these issues see Chapter 9, Israel and Palestine, in Irwin, C. J., *The People's Peace*, CreateSpace, Scotts Valley, CA, (2012).

Table 2. Reasons for the Northern Ireland Conflict

People from different communities often hold very different views about the causes of the conflict in Northern Ireland. Please indicate which ones you consider to be 'Very Significant' 'Significant', 'Of Some Significance', 'Of Little Significance' or 'Of No Significance' at all.

Percentage 'Very Significant'	All NI	Protestant	Catholic	DUP	UUP	Alliance	SDLP	Sinn Féin
The Irish Republican Army and their use of violence.	68	87	45	86	87	80	60	20
All paramilitary groups and their use of violence.	61	67	56	52	69	78	68	30
The Loyalist paramilitaries and their use of violence.	55	53	57	37	55	77	68	37
The failure of government and the security forces to deal with terrorism.	48	56	34	58	67	33	39	24
The sectarian division of Northern Ireland politics.	47	30	66	17	32	44	72	59
The failures of Northern Ireland politicians.	46	31	59	29	27	57	63	50
The Lack of equality and continued discrimination.	43	21	71	29	15	25	75	69
A lack of respect for the people of the 'other' tradition.	43	30	57	17	33	42	66	43
Unaccountable and secretive government.	40	31	52	45	26	25	55	48
The Republic's territorial claim on Northern Ireland.	38	53	21	60	57	31	16	24
The continued British presence on the island of Ireland.	32	17	51	23	14	27	44	73
The failure to provide a police service acceptable to all.	32	9	62	7	9	17	65	70
Segregated education.	30	25	31	27	23	33	35	23
The Republic of Ireland's involvement in Northern Ireland.	29	42	16	61	41	12	11	18
Segregated public housing.	28	23	33	28	18	25	35	25
The British Army and their use of violence.	24	6	48	6	5	17	47	52
The British Government's pursuit of a political settlement.	22	20	23	20	22	14	22	27
The prominent role of the Roman Catholic Church.	21	29	10	40	28	13	7	16
The 'Established Church' in Britain and the Orange Order.	18	14	21	17	11	12	19	29

Lesson 7 - Prioritising the elements of a conflict

Peace Building Problem
Each party to a conflict will not take the issues and concerns of other parties seriously. In particular they believe that the complaints put forward by other parties - particularly those directed at themselves - are little more than political rhetoric designed to ferment discord and distrust between their respective communities. The issues, concerns and complaints, they believe, are not genuine and therefore do not need to be addressed as part of a negotiated settlement.

Northern Ireland Experience
The party negotiators were invited to list what they believed to be the most significant causes of the Northern Ireland conflict. In practice when one party raised an issue of concern to their own community in a draft the next round of consultations stimulated a series of counter concerns from opposition parties. For example when Republicans proposed 'The British presence on the island of Ireland' as a problem Unionists countered with 'The Republic's involvement in Northern Ireland affairs' and so on. Social issues, like segregated education and housing, tended to be introduced by the smaller centre parties as was 'The failures of Northern Ireland politicians'. The question is given in Table 2 listing all the suggestions and results for Northern Ireland as a whole, Protestants, Catholics and each of the major political parties expressed as a percentage of those who said the 'cause' was 'Very Significant'.

Peace Making Best Practice
Get all the parties to a conflict to list the elements of the conflict, as seen from their point of view, in mutually acceptable neutral terms and test them against public opinion to see which issues are genuine concerns of the respective communities and which are not.

Israel and Palestine
Most of the polling done on the Middle East conflict is done in one community or state or another for the consumption of the people and politicians in those communities or states and their counterparts in Washington and other capitols. The polling is not generally done to inform Israeli and Palestinian citizens exactly what each other's priorities are for peace and how best to get there. It is not an on-going dialogue between the conflicting parties but more commonly a statement of their respective negotiating positions. Israelis and Palestinians live in their separate 'bubbles' maintained through the barriers of security walls, checkpoints,

different languages and separate lives. A successful peace process must necessarily bridge these gaps and the 2009 Irwin/OneVoice poll attempted to do this. The respective problems of each community were prioritised (Tables 3 and 4) but unlike Northern Ireland this program of public opinion research and public diplomacy was terminated, the problems were not addressed and the peace process failed.

Table 3. Top 5 of 15 problems of 'substance' for Israelis and Palestinians to negotiate

	Palestinian per cent	Very Significant	Israel per cent	Very Significant
1st	Establishing an independent sovereign state of Palestine	97	Security for Israel	77
2nd	The rights of refugees	95	Agreement on the future of Jerusalem	68
3rd	Agreement on the future of Jerusalem	94	Rights to natural resources	62
4th	Agreement on managing Holy sites	91	Agreement on managing Holy sites	57
5th	Security for Palestine	90	Agreeing borders for Israel and Palestine	49

Table 4. Top 5 of 56 problems of 'process' for Israelis and Palestinians to resolve

	Palestinian per cent	Very Significant	Israeli per cent	Very Significant
1st	The freedom of Palestinians from occupation/Israeli rule	94	Terror has reinforced the conflict	65
2nd	The settlements	89	Maintaining a Jewish majority in Israel	62
3rd	The substandard living conditions of the people in Gaza	88	Incitement to hatred	52
4th	The security wall	88	Weak Palestinian government	52
5th	The Independence of the Palestinian economy	87	Islamic extremists are changing a political war into a religious war	52

Lesson 8 - Prioritising the elements of a solution

Peace Building Problem
Politicians like to make peace deals. It can help to win elections. But easily made peace agreements that do not deal with the issues at the heart of a conflict are probably 'not worth the paper they are written on' and may well be broken 'before the ink is dry'. Beware of strangers bearing peace deals especially if their popularity is slipping at home.

Northern Ireland Experience
The party negotiators were invited to list their solutions for the problems drafted in Lesson 7 but where there had been 19 problems there were now only 17 'steps towards a lasting peace'.[25] Some 'steps' were redundant. As before Unionists tended to focus on security issues and decommissioning. Republicans and Nationalists on equality issues and reform of the police service. Again the centre parties could be relied upon to deal with social issues that the major parties considered to be less important for an agreement although perhaps essential as part of an effective peace process. Interestingly the general public agreed with the centre parties sometimes placing such matters higher on their list of priorities than 'Reformed and shared government'. The question is given in Table 5 listing all the suggestions and results for Northern Ireland as a whole, Protestants, Catholics and each of the major political parties expressed as a percentage of those who said the 'step' was 'Essential'.

Peace Making Best Practice
For every element of the conflict raised as a concern ask the parties to propose a potential solution. Rank these 'solutions' in their order of priority for each community and party to the conflict. Make sure everyone's top priorities are included in the settlement or it will most probably unravel and try to address all the issues raised as part of an on-going peace process.

---

[25] C. J. Irwin, 'Steps we need to take to win peace', *Belfast Telegraph*, Saturday, January 10th, (1998).

Table 5. Steps towards a lasting peace in Northern Ireland

As steps needed to help secure a lasting peace please indicate which of the following options you consider to be 'Essential', 'Desirable', 'Acceptable', 'Tolerable' or 'Unacceptable'?

Percentage 'Essential'	All NI	Protestant	Catholic	DUP	UUP	Alliance	SDLP	Sinn Féin
Disband all paramilitary groups.	70	70	66	45	79	76	85	39
Stronger and effective anti-terrorist measures.	57	69	39	66	77	61	48	22
A Bill of Rights that guarantees equality for all.	54	37	77	17	40	60	82	74
A Bill of Rights that protects the culture of each community.	49	36	67	26	40	41	71	63
A right to choose integrated education.	43	35	53	26	39	50	59	47
Politics without a sectarian division.	43	31	58	17	37	47	62	52
A right to choose integrated housing.	39	30	50	18	34	48	52	46
The Republic ends their claim on Northern Ireland.	38	63	7	74	68	25	6	14
Completely reform the police service.	34	7	70	5	6	8	70	86
Open government and Freedom of Information Act.	33	24	47	14	25	23	53	41
Return the army to their barracks.	31	8	60	11	7	19	60	77
Separate politics and religion in Northern Ireland.	27	31	20	28	28	37	19	19
End the Anglo-Irish Agreement.	24	36	10	49	40	6	7	14
Separate politics and religion in the Republic.	24	30	15	33	30	30	13	13
Reformed and shared government.	21	12	32	4	11	25	39	21
British withdrawal from Northern Ireland.	20	1	47	1	1	9	36	70
Integrate Northern Ireland into the UK.	20	35	4	44	41	8	3	5

Israel and Palestine

Table 6 from the 2009 Irwin/OneVoice poll lists the top 5 priorities for moving the peace process forward in both Israeli and Palestinian terms. Gilad Shalit has now been released (3rd item on the Israeli list), as have many Palestinian prisoners (5th on their list). Most of the other items on these two lists are 'doable' if the parties have a mind to and certainly would be possible on a 'quid pro quo' basis. But negotiations between Israel and Palestine are not managed with the support of a comprehensive program of public opinion research and public diplomacy aimed at achieving a peace settlement. They are not systematically addressing these issues of process so that they can move on to the critical matters of substance.

Table 6. Top 5 of 70 solutions of 'process' for Israelis and Palestinians to resolve

Palestinian per cent Essential or Desirable	Per Cent	Israeli per cent Essential or Desirable	Per Cent
1st Remove check points	100	Stop all suicide/attacks against civilians	90
2nd Lift the siege of Gaza	99	Stop firing rockets from Gaza	87
3rd Israel should freeze settlements as a first step to deal with the settlements	98	Release Gilad Shalit	85
4th Fatah and Hamas should reconcile their differences before negotiations	98	Prohibit all forms of incitement to hatred	81
5th Release Palestinian political prisoners in Israeli prisons	98	Achieve peace through negotiation	79

Lesson 9 - Setting the procedural parameters for a peace process

Peace Building Problem

Before an agreement can be reached 'shape of the table' decisions have to be made about who is eligible to negotiate, how decisions will be made in the negotiations, who will chair the negotiations, pay for them and where they will be held and last, but by no means least, if there is to be a referendum who is eligible to vote.

Northern Ireland Experience

Many of the procedural issues were settled by the British and Irish governments before the polls began. The parties to the Belfast negotiations held in Stormont Castle were elected on a proportional basis. The first ten got in. This ensured participation by parties with both Loyalist and Republican paramilitary connections. The two governments also favoured the John Hume/SDLP proposal of a referendum in both the North and South of Ireland at the same time, Sinn Féin wanted an all 'island of Ireland' referendum while Unionists preferred leaving it up to the Northern Ireland electorate alone. On 12 September 1997 the results of a poll exploring these and other related procedural issues was published in the *Belfast Telegraph*.[26] People wanted a referendum, they wanted the Stormont Talks to keep going even if Sinn Féin walked out (they didn't) and they wanted the largest Unionist and Nationalist parties to stay in (they did). The only workable compromise on who should vote in a Referendum appeared to be the John Hume/SDLP formula although Northern Ireland Protestants considered the Republic of Ireland vote to be of little or no relevance. However, by subsequently including changes to the Republic's constitution in that vote its importance, for everyone, was substantially increased. Northern Ireland Catholics also wanted any deal made to be supported by a majority in both communities. This was done in the system of party voting adopted in the Stormont Talks and also in the way the polls were analysed. Unionists favoured a simple majority and this is how the Northern Ireland referendum was calculated. So in a way everyone got a bit of what they wanted. Perhaps the most significant contribution made by the polls at this point in the proceedings was to help bring these technical issues into the public discourse and the fact that the people required far fewer preconditions than their political leaders. The people simply wanted them 'to get on with it'.

---

[26] C. J. Irwin, 'The people's vote', *Belfast Telegraph*, Friday, September 12th, (1997).

Peace Making Best Practice
Use public opinion polls to both test the various options for the design of the political negotiations as well as structuring the sampling, demographics and mode of analysis of the data collected in the polls to mirror the decision making processes that are adopted.

Israel and Palestine
The procedures for negotiating a peace agreement between Israel and Palestine are quite simply 'not fit for purpose'. They are 'off-again/on-again' between the political elites of the Prime Minister's office in Israel and the President's office in Palestine with the sometimes intervention of the US President's representative to the Middle East when one is appointed. The procedures of this peace process are set as much by the electoral cycle in America as they are by the necessities of peace in the region. None of this would matter if the political elites were negotiating in good faith and doing their duty for all the peoples who look to them for a successful outcome to their deliberations. But this is not the case. Every aspect of the Israel/Palestine negotiations needs reform with input - directly or indirectly - from all the parties to the conflict, intense negotiations in Jerusalem and elsewhere as may be required and independent monitoring of breaches of international law by the parties to the negotiations. This list could be much longer. Critically the 2009 Irwin/OneVoice poll focused on procedural issues, which were much easier to resolve then questions of substance. The publics in both Israel and Palestine wanted far more effective procedures than those on offer, but their wishes have been denied.[27]

---

[27] Irwin, C. J., Israel and Palestine: Public Opinion, Public Diplomacy and Peace Making. Part 2. Process, *www.Peacepolls.org*, April, (2009).

Lesson 10 - Setting the substantive parameters for a settlement

Peace Building Problem
Real peace agreements that attempt to address all the major problems at the heart of a conflict are necessarily complex dealing, as they must, with issues ranging from policing and human rights through electoral and constitutional reform to questions of amnesty and support for victims. Nothing substantive can be left out and the respective electorates have to vote 'yes' for an agreement that is necessarily a compromise and that does not deliver on all the promises made by their respective political leaders.

Northern Ireland Experience
The drafting of all the detailed questions for the 'In Search of a Settlement' poll took almost a year. While these questions were being agreed two polls were run in the spring and autumn of 1997 dealing with procedural issues. The third December poll of that year, published in the *Belfast Telegraph* on 10,[28] 12,[29] 13[30] and 14[31] January 1998, was timed to give a lift to the Stormont Talks after the Christmas break. While most people took a summer recess the negotiators worked on the polls and when they took a New Year holiday this poll was being analysed and prepared for publication. The questionnaire went through about a dozen drafts to produce a 22-page booklet that the interviewee filled out at home. The data produced were enormous dealing with public opinion on every major aspect of the Belfast Agreement: causes of the conflict and solutions, human rights, policing, an assembly, North/South bodies, East/West bodies, constitutional reform, a referendum, implementation, general preferences for a 'package' and a section on demographics. The general public were now very well informed about all the issues that had to be decided. The parties, governments and chair had detailed reports on public

---

[28] C. J. Irwin, 'Reforming RUC quite 'acceptable'', *Belfast Telegraph*, Saturday, January 10th, (1998). C. J. Irwin, 'Protecting the rights of the people', *Belfast Telegraph*, Saturday, January 10th, (1998). C. J. Irwin, 'Steps we need to take to win peace', *Belfast Telegraph*, Saturday, January 10th, (1998).
[29] C. J. Irwin, 'Why Ulster now wants to have new assembly', *Belfast Telegraph*, Monday, January 12th, (1998).
[30] C. J. Irwin, 'Feasibility and reality of north-south bodies', *Belfast Telegraph*, Tuesday, January 13th, (1998).
[31] C. J. Irwin, 'A Comprehensive Settlement', *Belfast Telegraph*, Wednesday, January 14th, (1998). C. J. Irwin, 'Constitutional Issues', *Belfast Telegraph*, Wednesday, January 14th, (1998). C. J. Irwin, 'What hope for Council of the Isles?', *Belfast Telegraph*, Wednesday, January 14th, (1998).

opinion as it related to each aspect of the agreement that they now had to make.[32] No one had a good excuse not to 'do the business' and negotiations got under way in earnest.

Peace Making Best Practice
Never be afraid to include any serious issue raised at the drafting stage. With explanatory preambles and the careful use of non-technical terms most issues can be explored with the public in carefully pre-tested booklet style take home questionnaires. Even if a question has to be dropped because it is too esoteric or just plain unhelpful its inclusion at the drafting stage will have raised the issue with the party negotiators and allowed them to wrestle with it.

Israel and Palestine
This is not being done in Israel and Palestine, as part of the formal negotiations, because they have not resolved the procedural issues that will allow the formal negotiations to proceed without interruption. The major points of an informal peace agreement negotiated as part of the *Geneva Accord*[33] are regularly tested against public opinion.[34] But the 'Devil is in the detail' and those details are not being explored with a view to resolving them as was done in Northern Ireland. This could be done informally as part of an on-going informal peace process but the Israeli and Palestinian people have been disenfranchised while their leaders and the key players in the international community concern themselves with electoral politics.[35]

---

[32] C. J. Irwin, *In Search of a Settlement, Summary Tables of Principal Statistical Results*, Institute of Irish Studies, The Queen's University of Belfast, January (1998).
[33] Geneva Accord available at: http://www.geneva-accord.org/
[34] Geneva Accord polls available at: http://www.geneva-accord.org/mainmenu/polls/
[35] For a review of these issues see Chapter 9, Israel and Palestine, in Irwin, C. J., *The People's Peace*, CreateSpace, Scotts Valley, CA, (2012).

Lesson 11 - Developing a common language and neutral terms for the drafting of a settlement

Peace Building Problem
During a conflict the language of political rhetoric and in particular the names of institutions, events and places develop separately within each community to produce distinctive vocabularies, symbols and meanings that are part of their different identities. But a settlement requires one agreed terminology that transcends the polarised and sometimes inflammatory vocabularies of the various communities and parties to a conflict.

Northern Ireland Experience
The detailed drafting of the 'In Search of a Settlement' questionnaire did not only facilitate the formulation of issues but also the development of a common language and terms acceptable to all parties. The methodology of requiring all parties to agree the questions demanded nothing less. Both sides had to adjust their rhetoric, at least for the purposes of an agreement. For example Republicans liked to refer to the Republic of Ireland as the 26 counties, Northern Ireland as the 6 counties and the whole island together as the 32 county Ireland or Eire as none of these terms implied partition. On the other hand Unionists wanted to use the terms 'Northern Ireland' and 'Republic of Ireland' as they recognised partition. Although these terms tended to be used for international legal reasons most parties also agreed to use the terms 'North of Ireland', 'South of Ireland' or simply 'North' and 'South' as well as 'Island of Ireland' for the both together. Similarly the idea of having a 'Council of the British Isles' had been floated around for some years by Unionists. This Council would be comprised of representatives from England, Scotland, Wales, Northern Ireland and the Republic of Ireland. But the Republic was not 'British' although many maps referred to this group of islands, off the North West coast of Continental Europe, as the 'British Isles'. Providing the term 'British' was dropped the concept was acceptable and the 'Council of the Isles' was born and subsequently got drafted into the Belfast Agreement.

Peace Making Best Practice
Draft, draft and redraft the questions to be run in each poll with the political contact group until a consensus is reached with regards to all terminology to be used. Necessarily inflammatory and partisan language will have to be replaced with neutral terms if the answers to the survey questions are not to produce biased results that would prejudice the outcome of the research.

Israel and Palestine

When I first started to extend my work on the Northern Ireland peace process to Israel and Palestine in the 1990s Israelis strongly objected to the use of the term 'Palestinian'. At conferences in Israel the preferred term was Arab, and Israelis who used the term Palestinian would open themselves up to severe criticism from their colleagues. This situation has changed over the years with Palestinian now far more acceptable than it was, but separate terminologies sometimes still had to be used in the 2009 Irwin/OneVoice poll. For example: 'West Bank and Gaza' in Israel and 'Palestinian or Occupied Territories' in Palestine. Peace in the Middle East requires a common language and every agreed common term brings the conflicting parties one step closer to a comprehensive peace agreement. However difficult the negotiations we never ran a question in Northern Ireland with two separate vocabularies.

Lesson 12 - Searching for and mapping out 'middle' and 'common' ground

Peace Building Problem
One man's middle ground is another man's surrender. Inevitably, everyone, except perhaps the talk's chairman, views a fair compromise as a sell out to the other side.

Northern Ireland Experience
Once all the questions are drafted to everyone's satisfaction then each issue should contain a series of options or choices for which the informant can indicate their preference. In the first poll done in this series people were asked to rank order their first, second and third choice and so on. This worked reasonably well up to a maximum of about eight choices but it got progressively more difficult and slow. In the second poll those being interviewed were asked to say which options they considered to be 'Desirable', 'Acceptable', 'Tolerable' or 'Unacceptable' and in subsequent polls 'Essential' was also added in as a first choice. This five-point scale worked very well indeed. It was simple to administer in the field if the same style was used throughout the questionnaire. Adding more options didn't make answering the questions more difficult and analysing the results produced easy to understand information that clearly indicated how much each community wanted or did not like each option. For example, here are the results for the controversial North/South bodies options published in the *Belfast Telegraph* on 13 January 1998.[36] Unionists did not want them at all or with as few powers as possible. Republicans wanted them to have strong powers that would effectively make them a government of Ireland as a whole. The polls indicated that the Protestant community would accept North/South bodies with powers of consultation, co-operation and administration providing these powers did not exceed the authority of the respective governments, North and South, that had set them up. Catholics required these bodies as part of an agreement and they got them within the limitations acceptable to the Protestant community (Figure 1).

Peace Making Best Practice
Test solutions to problems as a series of graded options that span the issue being raised from the radical position of one party through the centre ground to the radical positions of others. Inevitably the fair compromise, as

---

[36] C. J. Irwin, 'Feasibility and reality of north-south bodies', *Belfast Telegraph*, Tuesday, January 13th, (1998).

well as points of agreement, will receive the greatest cross community support, objectively measured and not subjectively perceived.

Figure 1. On matters of mutual interest North/South bodies should:

	Essential	Desirable	Acceptable	Tolerable	Unacceptable

Be required to consult.

	Essential	Desirable	Acceptable	Tolerable	Unacceptable	
Protestant	16	17	25	13	29	
Catholic	56			24	15	3 2

Be required to co-operate.

	Essential	Desirable	Acceptable	Tolerable	Unacceptable	
Protestant	16	19	19	14	32	
Catholic	57			25	14	3 1

Have powers to administer laws made by the separate governments in the North and the South of Ireland.

	Essential	Desirable	Acceptable	Tolerable	Unacceptable	
Protestant	3	14	16	18	49	
Catholic	36		31	21	5	7

Have powers to develop and execute forward planning for the island of Ireland as a whole.

	Essential	Desirable	Acceptable	Tolerable	Unacceptable	
Protestant	3	9	13	12	63	
Catholic	46			30	16	4 4

Have powers to make laws which would apply to the island of Ireland as a whole.

	Essential	Desirable	Acceptable	Tolerable	Unacceptable	
Protestant	3	5	12	10	70	
Catholic	44		24	20	7	5

Or there should not be any North/South bodies with any powers or functions.

	Essential	Desirable	Acceptable	Tolerable	Unacceptable
Protestant	27	13	13	18	29
Catholic	4 3 8	16	69		

Israel and Palestine
Israeli and Palestinian peace researchers are reluctant to run polls that deal with the extreme positions of the two communities and thus expose the true feelings of their electorates on such issues. But unless this is done in both communities together the possibilities of establishing the necessity of carefully crafted compromises cannot be clearly demonstrated in contrast to those extreme positions. Additionally, when research is done in this way, extremist politicians can make the point that their proposals were not tested against public opinion, allowing them to dismiss the results of the research as irrelevant. Finally, without input from real negotiators the finer points of compromise cannot get drafted and tested against public opinion so progress in the peace process towards new accommodations cannot be made with the aid of such polls.

Lesson 13 - Testing the viability of radical proposals against public opinion

Peace Building Problem
Some parties and, at the very least, some members of some parties remain wedded to the radical views of their constituency as the best solution to everyone's problems. They simply will not accept that a compromise with cross community support is the only viable solution and way forward.

Northern Ireland Experience
In addition to testing radical proposals as options alongside options for compromise and common ground in all the public opinion poll questions, extreme Republican and extreme Unionist solutions were also tested against the emergent Belfast Agreement shortly before it was made. The Unionist alternative to a comprehensive settlement was published in the *Belfast Telegraph* on Tuesday 31 March 1998.[37] They wanted a devolved government like Scotland or Wales and for Northern Ireland to remain part of the United Kingdom. A simple majority of the population said 'Yes' to this proposal but significantly a higher percentage preferred the Belfast Agreement style comprehensive settlement from both communities, and a majority of Catholics did not wish to remain in the UK. The Republican alternative was published the following day, Wednesday 1 April.[38] Although a slim majority of Protestants would accept police reform they would not accept an 'all island of Ireland' body to manage policing. Having the people of Northern Ireland decide their constitutional status was acceptable to both communities but Protestants would not accept having their fait placed before an 'all island of Ireland' vote and almost everyone, except Sinn Féin, wanted a regional assembly. That day the headline read 'Little support for SF agenda'.

Peace Making Best Practice
From time to time test radical proposals against public opinion but be sure to get the radicals involved in the exercise with the questions drafted to their satisfaction. Inevitably such proposals will only receive support from their own constituency and even then that support may not be as strong as they might suppose. Most people can recognise an honourable compromise when they see it - and when they don't.

---

[37] C. J. Irwin, 'Alternatives to a comprehensive settlement', *Belfast Telegraph*, Tuesday, March 31st, (1998).
[38] C. J. Irwin, 'Little support for SF agenda', *Belfast Telegraph*, Wednesday, April 1st, (1998).

Israel and Palestine

This kind of exposure of radical solutions from extremist politicians and their polarized constituencies can only be an effective tool for positive public diplomacy when the results of such polls are published in the media of all the parties to the conflict at the same time. But Israelis and Palestinians live separate lives in segregated communities informed by their own media in their own languages, which in turn are serviced by their own news agencies. The necessities of a modern peace process and public diplomacy require the establishment of a comprehensive strategic communications strategy and joint news agency.[39]

---

[39] This was done in Kosovo and Serbia with the establishment of the 'Albanian-Serb Information Exchange Forum' available at:
http://www.cdsee.org/projects/albanian_serb_exchange_forum

Lesson 14 - Testing comprehensive agreements as a set of balanced compromises

Peace Building Problem

Not every part of an agreement can be settled as a search for common ground or even compromise. Some parts, which are very important to one party, will have to be 'horse traded' for other parts, equally important to other parties. The deal, as a whole, will inevitably contain a few victories and disappointments for each side to the conflict. Can the deal be sold?

Northern Ireland Experience

Yes the deal can be sold. If it is fair and has the potential to deliver peace, with all the benefits that can flow from that, then it will be acceptable. But it does have to be sold as the Northern Ireland polls and subsequent referendum campaign clearly demonstrated. The front-page headline of the *Belfast Telegraph* on 31 March 1998[40] read '77% SAY YES'. This result was for Northern Ireland as a whole in response to reading a six-point summary of the proposed settlement and being asked if they would support it if their political party also did. But in a follow up question this support fell to 50% if the support of their party was withdrawn. Clearly the deal could be done but the two governments would not be able to go over the heads of the parties. They would have to do it together. Two further points are worth noting here. Firstly the supporters of Loyalist and Republican parties with paramilitary associations had the greatest misgivings about a deal but they trusted their leadership and would follow them. Secondly when asked about each of the six points of the proposed agreement in turn many people who said 'Yes' to the package as a whole said 'No' to some of the parts of the deal they still did not like. People were willing to compromise, in a big way, for the sake of an honourable settlement.

Peace Making Best Practice

Test the comprehensive agreement to be put to the people in a referendum as a complete set of its major points and then test each element separately. The whole will be greater than the sum of its parts and will probably be 'acceptable' as a comprehensive agreement although individual issues may well remain contentious or even 'unacceptable' in isolation from the total package.

---

[40] P. Connolly, '77% SAY YES', *Belfast Telegraph*, Tuesday, March 31st, (1998).

Israel and Palestine

Following the test of the Belfast Agreement as a 'package' in 1998 Israeli and Palestinian pollsters started using this technique to test the Clinton/Geneva settlement framework in 2003.[41] They have produced an excellent time line analysis of support for these accords with 58% of Israelis and 50% of Palestinians saying they would vote 'yes' in December 2011.[42] But that is as far as it goes. Without a modern peace process that also deals with all the public opinion, public diplomacy and procedural problems that stand in the way of real negotiations the results of these polls are of little more than academic interest.

---

[41] Geneva Accord polls available at: ttp://www.geneva-accord.org/mainmenu/new-joint-poll-december-2011-support-for-the-geneva-initiative-significantly-increased
[42] Joint Israel Palestinian Poll, December 2011 available at:
http://www.pcpsr.org/survey/polls/2011/p42ejoint.html#attitueds1

Keeping the Peace Process 'On Tack'

Lesson 15 - Scheduling the decision making process

Peace Building Problem
The 'horses have been brought to water' but they simply will not drink. Everyone knows what the compromise is, the shape of the deal is clear, but no one will take the plunge. 'After you sir' - 'No after you'. Without a decision being taken confidence in the peace process starts to fade, a political vacuum forms and violence creeps back onto the streets.

Northern Ireland Experience
The work with party negotiators to design the first questionnaire began in January of 1997, data collection for the first poll was undertaken between 12 and 22 March and the results were published in the *Belfast Telegraph* on 7, 8, and 9 April. That is about two months for the design of the poll and three weeks for interviews, analysis and writing up. Critically this poll was published to deal with procedural problems holding up the Stormont talks prior to the imminent May 1st general election. A change of government was expected and it was hoped the poll would help to clear the way for a fresh start to the negotiations. In particular it was intended that the results should stimulate public debate but care was taken not to publish too close to voting day so as to avoid accusations of political interference. From this time on, until the signing of the Belfast Agreement, questionnaire design was ongoing particularly when the Stormont talks were in recess. The second poll was published on Thursday 11 and Friday 12 September before an Ulster Unionist Party meeting on Saturday 13 September at which they had to decide if they would go into talks with Sinn Féin on Monday 14 September. If they decided 'No' the talks would collapse. They decided 'Yes'. The third poll, that dealt with all the substantive elements of an agreement, was published on 10, 12, 13 and 14 January to provide 'food for thought' after the Christmas and New Year break (but no holiday for the pollsters!). Deals were made and a 'package' was tested in the fourth poll against public opinion between 12 - 20 March and published on 31 March. The Belfast Agreement was made on Good Friday 10 April 1998. The fifth poll published on 3 and 4 March 1999, created an opportunity for new negotiations on the question of decommissioning and the sixth poll published on 26 and 27 October dealt with issues raised in the Mitchell Review which was brought to a successful conclusion a week later. The seventh poll, like the second poll, was published just days before an Ulster Unionist Party meeting called to decide whether or not to take the Party back into the Executive with Sinn Féin. They did.

Peace Making Best Practice

Timing is everything. Arrange with the parties to the negotiations when the results of a poll should be published so that the publication event will precede the decisions to be made in the negotiations by an appropriate period of days or weeks - not longer. Also get the detailed statistical reports to the parties at the same time to both assist them with the decisions they must make and allow them to give informed answers to the press. All of this will help to raise expectations for a conclusion to this part of the peace process. A good talk's chairman will seize the moment.

Israel and Palestine

With all of this experience in mind the fieldwork for the Irwin/OneVoice poll was undertaken as soon as it was known that Obama had won the US Presidency in 2008 and George Mitchell would be appointed his Special Envoy to the Middle East. The objective of this first poll was to explore all possible options for moving the peace process forward when Obama took office in 2009. Although this initiative was quite successful it was not followed up with a program of pro-active peace polling leaving the public opinion and public diplomacy field open to Israeli partisan polling that undermined the peace process by focusing on the settlement issue in an unhelpful way.[43] To say that those working on the polling and public diplomacy should cooperate closely with those responsible for the negotiations is an understatement. It needs to be much more than this. It should be a close collaboration if peace is to be achieved. In Israel and Palestine the polling undertaken in support of the peace process most commonly 'follows the curve' when it should be 'ahead of the curve' helping to set the agenda not commenting on it.

---

[43] For a discussion of these issues see Chapter 9, Israel and Palestine, in Irwin, C. J., *The People's Peace*, CreateSpace, Scotts Valley, CA., (2012).

Lesson 16 - Establishing leader, party, public and international confidence in the decisions to be made

Peace Building Problem
At the moment of decision people start to lose their nerve. Is this a good idea or is it political suicide?

Northern Ireland Experience
Each poll contained a wide range of questions dealing with issues left over from the previous poll; the beginnings of new questions to be explored in greater depth in future polls; contextual 'how do you feel about' questions; ordering priorities and so on. But each poll also contained a set of questions designed specifically to help resolve particular problems that arose at that point in the peace process. In the first poll the most critical issue to be addressed was decommissioning. People did not want the negotiations to be stopped. If there was a problem they wanted it dealt with by a subcommittee. In the second poll all the objections to negotiations had to be dealt with. Critically Ulster Unionist supporters wanted their party to be in the negotiations with Sinn Féin. The third poll was designed to provide detailed information about public opinion on all the different parts of the agreement that had to be made. The agreement took shape and was tested as a 'package' in the fourth poll. Critically the parties knew before they cut a deal that they could win a referendum. They did. As well as demonstrating continued support for the Belfast Agreement in the three post agreement polls the first of these polls, the fifth poll, explored various options for overcoming the problem of decommissioning and new negotiations were initiated. The sixth poll dealt with these problems again in the Mitchell Review but also included a lot of questions about how people felt about the failing peace process. People wanted action and the new institutions of government were established. In the seventh poll the concept of 'placing arms beyond use' was tested against public opinion and shown to be generally 'acceptable'. But it was close. Although the Ulster Unionist Council decided to go back into government with Sinn Féin on this basis the vote was only 459 in favour to 403 against.

Peace Making Best Practice
Content is as important as timing. Agree with the parties which questions are going to be run in which poll. The person or team running the poll must have their 'finger on the political pulse' and should know what results are required by paying close attention to people on the street, news reports, radio talk shows, the press and most importantly their private discussions

with the party negotiators. Poll results cannot be 'fixed', but they must be relevant and the analysis must draw conclusions appropriate to the needs of the day.

Israel and Palestine

In addition to being the most researched conflict in the world Israel and Palestine are now probably the most polled as surveys of public opinion become an increasingly more significant element of democratic political culture all over the world. But quantity does not necessarily mean quality and certainly does not equate with polling as a constructive part of a peace process. In Northern Ireland the BBC and other news media were running polls but the peace polls there were simply bigger, better and critically more relevant to the resolution of the conflict than any of the other polls. They set a standard which, in time, the other pollsters had to meet or be dismissed as of little relevance. A well-managed program of peace polls does not only help resolve problems at the centre of a conflict it also raises the game for everyone else. The polling undertaken in Israel and Palestine lacks coordination so the good work that does get done is drowned out by the noise of other pollsters whose work is frequently of very poor quality or partisan. The analysts in Washington, Oslo, Geneva and other Western capitols may be very pleased with the public opinion surveys they commission but they are loosing the public diplomacy war where and when it matters.[44]

---

[44] For example although the Geneva Accord website lists the polls that draw conclusions in support of negotiations and a peace agreement between Israel and Palestine they have edited out the partisan polls that oppose their initiative. This would be understandable if they were winning the public diplomacy war. But they are not. The partisan pollsters have won as illustrated by this sequence of polls:

- 'Survey: Israeli Jews oppose settlement freeze and evacuation of outposts' (*Israel News:* Lerner, A., June 4, 2009)
- 'Dahaf Institute Poll: Majority Of Israelis Support Obama's Settlement Policy' (*Yedioth Ahronoth:* Kadmon, June 5, 2009)
- 'Poll: 56% of Israelis back settlement construction' (*Associated Press:* June 12, 2009)
- 'J Street blasts 'distorted' poll that says Israelis against settlement freeze' (*Haaretz Service:* June12, 2009)
- ''Jerusalem Post'/Smith Poll: Only 6% of Israelis see US gov't as pro-Israel' (The *Jerusalem Post:* Hofman, G., and Smith Research/Jerusalem Post Poll, June 19, 2009)
- 'Poll: Israelis oppose full settlement freeze 69%:27%, only 6% say Obama favours Israel' (*Independent Media Review Analysis:* June 19, 2009)
- 'Netanyahu's Defiance of U.S. Resonates at Home: Polls Show Resistance to Settlement Freeze' (*The Washington Post:* Howard Schneider, August 19, 2009)

(The Geneva Accords polls can be accessed at: http://www.geneva-accord.org/mainmenu/polls/)

Lesson 17 - Supporting pro-Agreement parties and the people's decision

Peace Building Problem
Those opposed to an agreement, even when it has been endorsed by the people in a referendum, continue to criticise it from their own constituency's point of view as at least unworkable and more probably unfair. Slowly they try to erode support for the agreement in the hope that what they think was lost in the referendum can be reversed in future elections.

Northern Ireland Experience
All ten parties elected to participate in the negotiation of the Belfast Agreement were treated equally and had the same rights of access to the process of designing and running the public opinion polls as part of the Northern Ireland peace process. However, after the agreement was reached I was asked if I would like to help the pro-agreement 'YES Campaign', but the funders, the Joseph Rowntree Charitable Trust, advised me not to do so as such an action could be considered political and thus might prejudice the independence of future research. However, after the referendum of 22 May 1998, in which a majority voted for the agreement, this restriction was relaxed and I worked with the pro-Agreement parties as required although all final reports continued to be made available to both pro and anti-agreement parties. At this point in the peace process it would have been difficult to work with the anti-agreement parties in good faith as they would have wished to introduce questions with the intention of undermining support for the agreement. Tracking support for the Belfast Agreement also became an essential part of the three post referendum polls as others were running polls that showed Protestant support to be slipping. Although many people were disappointed with the rate of progress with implementation and had 'second thoughts' about voting for such an agreement again they did want it to work. Some results from the Mitchell Review poll are given in Table 7.[45]

---

[45] C. J. Irwin, 'Guns, trust and the Agreement', *Belfast Telegraph*, Tuesday, October 26th, (1999).

Table 7. Support for the Belfast Agreement during the Mitchell Review

How did you vote in the referendum for the Belfast Agreement?

	All of NI	Protestant	Catholic	DUP	UUP	PUP	Alliance	SDLP	Sinn Fein
Yes	74%	64%	89%	32%	82%	85%	90%	96%	89%
No	26%	36%	11%	68%	18%	15%	10%	4%	11%

And if the Referendum was held today how would you vote?

	All of NI	Protestant	Catholic	DUP	UUP	PUP	Alliance	SDLP	Sinn Fein
Yes	65%	49%	88%	31%	56%	56%	79%	95%	90%
No	35%	51%	12%	69%	44%	44%	21%	5%	10%

Do you want the Belfast Agreement to work?

	All of NI	Protestant	Catholic	DUP	UUP	PUP	Alliance	SDLP	Sinn Fein
Yes	83%	72%	98%	50%	87%	91%	98%	98%	97%
No	17%	28%	2%	50%	13%	9%	2%	2%	3%

Peace Making Best Practice
Periodically run public opinion polls after an agreement is reached to demonstrate continued support for the agreement as both a deal that people would still vote for and more critically as a deal that they would like to see work.

Israel and Palestine
Since they were signed in 1993 support for the Oslo Accords has fallen away, year on year, in both Israel and Palestine, because they have not been fully implemented and because they have not delivered peace. For example by May 2004 only 26% of Israelis supported the Accords while only 18% believed they would deliver peace.[46] However, from a peace polls and public diplomacy perspective the critical question that should have also been asked is 'do you want the Accords to work?' In practice all these questions should be asked together in both communities on a regular basis to inform all the parties to such agreements exactly where their support is and where it is under threat in both social and political demographic detail.

---

[46] The Tami Steinmetz Center for Peace Research, War and Peace Index available at: http://www.spirit.tau.ac.il/xeddexcms008/manage.asp?siteID=5&lang=2

Lesson 18 - Monitoring the implementation of an agreement

Peace Building Problem
Implementing an agreement can be as difficult, or even more difficult, than reaching the agreement itself, especially when the agreement required significant compromises to be made by all the parties involved. Those opposed to the agreement do all they can to frustrate its implementation by employing the strategy of 'death by a thousand cuts'.

Northern Ireland Experience
The Belfast Agreement had a two-year transition period built into it designed to allow for all the institutional and social changes required under the terms of the settlement to be implemented. But after 30 years of the 'Troubles' and arguably a civil war that hadn't been properly brought to a close since the 1920s a two-year transition period was just not quite long enough. Everyone started to relax after the deal was cut, most of the people involved with the negotiations were exhausted and the critiques of the deal started to 'sharpen their knives'. There were not meant to be any more polls but when it became clear that the agreement was starting to unravel some parties asked for them to be run again. Unlike previous polls these ones included a series of questions that asked people how they felt about the peace process and how satisfied they were with the implementation of the different parts of the agreement. They were worried about a return to violence and specific failures with implementation were clearly identifiable. The politicians got a bit of a 'cold shower' and points requiring urgent action were plainly visible in the statistics. On the one hand it was hoped that the politicians would have been able to work the agreement through their new institutions without the support of more polls. However, with the benefit of hindsight and four more polls done, it would probably have been best to keep the process going with a poll run about twice a year during the early years of implementation. In this way problems could have better been identified and dealt with before they reached crisis point.

Peace Making Best Practice
Periodically run public opinion polls after an agreement is reached to monitor levels of satisfaction with the implementation of its different parts and the social impact of the peace process in general. Require the relevant parties to take both timely and effective political action to address critical points of discontent and failure.

Israel and Palestine

Most of the peace agreements in the Middle East have not been fully implemented, the most prominent of these failures being the Oslo Accords. There is no regular testing of public satisfaction with its various provisions, in both Palestine and Israel, as a part of a collective responsibility for their implementation. Inevitably trust has broken down on both sides and without an effective remedy for these omissions entry into a new peace agreement will be significantly more difficult. A rigorous public appraisal of all past agreements using the same research instruments in both Israel and Palestine might be a good place to start.

Lesson 19 - Providing reports to the public to facilitate their involvement in the peace process

Peace Building Problem
Secret negotiations can leave the public 'in the dark' leading to mischievous speculation about the nature of the agreement or lack of progress in the talks. When an agreement is finally reached it contains quite a few surprises leading to more disinformation and the electorate are unprepared for a referendum when it comes.

Northern Ireland Experience
Throughout 1996 I published a series of articles on peace building in the *Belfast Telegraph*[47], which were the results of a public opinion survey undertaken by a team of researchers at Queen's University.[48] But in the spring of 1997 the *Belfast Telegraph* ran a rather disastrous phone in poll in which members of the Orange Order made sure the phone in vote was 'Yes' for their most controversial march of the year. As a consequence the editor of the *Belfast Telegraph* came in for much criticism from moderate politicians and he asked me if I could do a more scientific poll. This was done on the condition that the feature story could not be changed although they would retain editorial control of the front page. All the subsequent polls were published on this basis. The *Belfast Telegraph* had the largest circulation in the province and although it was considered to be a Unionist paper it was widely read in both communities and its editorial policy was pro-agreement. Several attempts were made to work with the broadcast media and other newspapers through a variety of deals and press releases. But all these attempts failed. The press releases were 'cherry picked', the broadcast media only wanted adversarial debates and newspapers from outside the province could not give detailed coverage to complex political issues that only those living in Northern Ireland could properly appreciate. The stories for the *Belfast Telegraph* were delivered a day or two before

---

[47] C. J. Irwin, 'Ulster People Could Decide Way Forward', *Belfast Telegraph*, Tuesday, December 3rd, (1996). C. J. Irwin, 'The FEC.... Fair To Meddling?' *Belfast Telegraph*, Wednesday, November 20th, (1996). C. J. Irwin, 'Hitting A Brick Wall', *Belfast Telegraph*, Tuesday, October 22nd, (1996). C. J. Irwin, 'Ulster Amnesty Rejected', *Belfast Telegraph*, Monday, September 30th, (1996). C. J. Irwin, 'The Battle For The Middle Ground', *Belfast Telegraph*, Thursday, September 12th, (1996). C. J. Irwin, 'Changing The Force Of Habit', *Belfast Telegraph*, Friday, August 2nd, (1996). C. J. Irwin, 'The Parade Question', *Belfast Telegraph*, Thursday, July 4th, (1996).
[48] T. Hadden, C. Irwin and F. Boal, 'Separation or sharing? the people's choice', Supplement with *Fortnight* 356, Belfast, December (1996).

publication to give the graphic artist time to produce the artwork for the tables of statistics and for the political editors to write their front-page story and occasional leader. The parties looked forward to the publication very much. They felt it helped to keep the grass roots of their constituencies informed and involved in the peace process. On the street, through their letterbox, in the Maze prison and at Parliament Buildings everyone got the story at the same time.

Peace Making Best Practice
Publish poll results and analysis in the popular press with a view to informing the public on the stage the negotiations have reached, the issues being discussed and the decisions that have to be made. When an agreement is finally reached the public will be ready to vote without the need for any unnecessary delay.

Israel and Palestine
Political analysts in both Israel and Palestine are well aware that the failure to prepare their respective publics for the compromises needed for a peace agreement was a major contributing factor to the breakdown of negotiations sponsored by the Clinton and subsequent US Administrations.[49] So why hasn't this problem been corrected? One possible answer to this question is that the parties to the conflict actually prefer the status quo to a peace agreement and its implementation but a more subtle and persuasive explanation in my view is that the bureaucracies running the peace process in Washington, Jerusalem and Ramallah are stuck in the political culture of all negotiations being undertaken 'behind closed doors'. But peace polls managed in collaboration with the negotiating parties can provide just the right balance of both confidentiality and public diplomacy as required. Negotiations between Israel and Palestine, it would seem, have fallen victim to the bureaucratic imperative of 'safety in secrecy'.

---

[49] Klein, M., Bar-Ilan University, Israel, *Failed Israeli and Palestinian Interactions*, Royal Irish Academy, Friday, 22 November, (2002). Irwin, C. J., *Public Opinion and the Politics of Peace Research: Northern Ireland, Balkans, Israel, Palestine, Cyprus, Muslim World and the 'War on Terror'*, Palestinian Centre for Policy and Survey Research and the Harry S. Truman Research Institute for the Advancement of Peace joint conference: Public Opinion, Democracy and Peace Making, Notre Dame of Jerusalem Centre, Jerusalem, May 22-23, (2006). Shamir, J. and Shikaki, K., *Palestinian and Israeli Public Opinion: The Public Imperative in the Second Intifada*, Indiana University Press, Bloomington and Indianapolis, (2010).

Lesson 20 - Providing reports to the parties to assist their decision-makers with their negotiations

Peace Building Problem
In the 'information age' detailed analysis and access to reliable up to date facts about all aspects of public opinion on a conflict are essential if informed decisions are to be made. A failure to provide accurate and timely information can lead to decisions not being made and opportunities lost.

Northern Ireland Experience
Some large national political parties do have specialist research departments with experts at the ready to analyse, digest and write memoranda on piles of statistical computer print out. But most of the Northern Ireland parties did not have these facilities available to them so reports were designed and printed to provide them with the key statistics in a way that was unbiased, informative and accessible. This was done by using the questionnaire itself as the basis for the structure of the report. Firstly the results for Northern Ireland as a whole were reproduced in each question where the informant would usually write in their answer. This would be followed by a community and political break down: Protestant, Catholic, Democratic Unionist Party (DUP), Ulster Unionist Party (UUP), Loyalist Parties (Ulster Democratic Party and/or Progressive Unionist Party), Alliance Party, Social Democratic and Labour Party (SDLP) and Sinn Féin. This order was deliberate flowing from politically more extreme Protestants and Unionists through the centre to politically more extreme Catholics, Nationalists and Republicans. Wherever possible all the results for a particular question were placed on a single page or, for more complex questions, the Northern Ireland, Protestant and Catholic results were placed on one page and the political party results on adjoining pages. The report, like the questionnaire, also contained a demographic section that gave a break down of the sample and party support in terms of gender, age and social class (coded from occupation). This section was particularly popular with party electoral strategists. But parties with less than about five per cent of the vote were not generally included in these reports, except for the 'which party do you support' question, as their samples were boarder line in terms of statistical significance without 'booster' or 'over-samples'. Finally a 'full copy' of the story delivered to the *Belfast Telegraph* was also given to the parties as it nearly always contained a number of analytical tables the newspaper would not have space to publish. The culture of each of the Northern Ireland parties was surprisingly different and as a result the parties used the statistical reports in different ways and to varying degrees

as a research tool for strategy development, negotiating device, public opinion/media resource or for grass roots constituency development and information. Very few compliments were received on the quality of these reports, however, if they were late and not delivered promptly on the day of publication of the *Belfast Telegraph* stories: then numerous complaints could be expected.

Peace Making Best Practice
In addition to reports in the popular press provide detailed statistical reports to all the parties to the negotiations with breakdowns of all questions by both political affiliation and religious, ethnic, racial, linguistic and national group as is appropriate. Be as helpful as possible. For example, demographic analysis of party support is generally also very welcome in terms of age, gender and social class.

Israel and Palestine
Because the Iriwn/OneVoice poll in Israel and Palestine had to be completed on a very restricted budget it was not possible to break down the samples into their smallest constituent demographic parts. This was a very serious omission. Typically extremist groups holding radical views are very small and it is not only important to know what these groups are thinking it is also very important, from a public diplomacy perspective, for everyone else to know how unrepresentative they are. For example, the members of the Irish Republican Army (IRA) who did not want to decommission their weapons, was only about 1 per cent of the Northern Irish population. It is absolutely essential that politicians making difficult decisions are given as much detailed information as possible by their researchers, which in turn requires sufficiently large enough samples and no editing out of relevant issues and questions before the polls are run. The questions they ask must be answered.

Conclusion

Lesson 21 - Providing reports to the international community to maintain their good offices

Peace Building Problem
The international community are not interested in lending their support to the resolution of the conflict because they have no strategic interest in the area and/or do not believe the conflict can be resolved.

Northern Ireland Experience
There was a time, perhaps during the Second World War, when Northern Ireland was of strategic interest to the United Kingdom. Indeed Ireland as a whole was of strategic interest then and Churchill was willing to settle the Northern Ireland problem in the Republic's favour if they were willing to enter the war in opposition to Germany. But world military and economic strategies changed with the advent of nuclear weapons and the creation of the North Atlantic Treaty Organisation and European Union. In this context Ireland, Britain and their close ally America, as well as the European Union, all wanted the Northern Ireland problem solved and all were willing to expend political capitol on a successful outcome. The people of Northern Ireland were very lucky, a lot of very influential people and powerful states cared about their situation and were willing to take the risk of getting involved in an apparently intractable conflict. But a successful settlement was the key; nobody wanted to be associated with failure. Although the results of the Northern Ireland polls were rarely reported beyond the pages of the *Belfast Telegraph* the detailed reports given to the parties were also given to the British and Irish governments and to the Office of the Independent Chairmen. Senator George Mitchell, the principle talks Chairman and Review facilitator, took a keen interest in the reports and frequently expressed the view in public that an agreement could be reached because that is what the people of Northern Ireland wanted.[50] In this way the polls probably helped to maintain the confidence of the good Senator in the peace process and no doubt, through him, the support of the then President of the United States of America, Bill Clinton.

Peace Making Best Practice
Try to publish reports of the polls in the newspapers of any ally who can lend their good offices to the resolution of the conflict and send detailed reports to key decision makers in the governments of such states. Given the interest in the resolution of the Northern Ireland problem it was not

---

[50] G. Mitchell, *Making Peace: The inside story of the making of the Good Friday Agreement* (London: William Heinemann, 1999).

necessary to send reports to other third parties but in many situations it may also be helpful to send detailed reports to both regional and global international organisations (IGOs) and non-governmental organisations (NGOs) in the hope that they too might be willing to lend their support to the achievement of a successful peace process.

Israel and Palestine
The problem for Israel and Palestine is that their conflict is probably the most significant conflict in the world, both in the region and for the major super powers, particularly the United States of America. As a consequence it is researched on an industrial scale marking it out as a major source of funding for the worlds peace industry. Unfortunately this unprecedented degree of international attention has proven counter productive to the resolution of the conflict. Reports from NGOs and IGOs to charitable and state funders emphasize their success when they are most assuredly failing, and continue to do so because they are reluctant to challenge the status quo when such challenges might prejudice the renewal of their grants and research contracts. In this circumstance NGOs and IGOs are encouraging what Palestinians call Normalization at the expense of conflict resolution. The solution to this problem, Lesson 21, is to implement Lessons 1 through 20.

Selected Bibliography

Irwin, C. J., *The People's Peace: 'Pax Populi, Pax Dei' - How Peace Polls are Democratizing the Peace Making Process,* CreateSpace, Scotts Valley, CA, (2012).

Irwin, C. J., *The People's Peace Process in Northern Ireland,* Palgrave MacMillan, Basingstoke and New York, (2002).

Mitchell, G., *Making Peace: The inside story of the making of the Good Friday Agreement,* London, William Heinemann, (1999).

Shamir, J. and Shikaki, K., *Palestinian and Israeli Public Opinion: The Public Imperative in the Second Intifada,* Indiana University Press, Bloomington and Indianapolis, (2010).

See Footnotes 1 through 50 for full references

Index

Printed in Great Britain
by Amazon